THE WRITER'S LIFE

Also by Julia Cameron

NONFICTION

The Artist's Way *(with Mark Bryan)*
The Artist's Way Morning Pages Journal
The Artist's Date Book
(illustrated by Elizabeth Cameron)
The Vein of Gold
The Right to Write
God Is No Laughing Matter
Supplies *(illustrated by Elizabeth Cameron)*
God Is Dog Spelled Backwards
(illustrated by Elizabeth Cameron)
Heartsteps
Blessings
Transitions
The Artist's Way at Work *(with Mark Bryan
and Catherine Allen)*
Money Drunk, Money Sober *(with Mark Bryan)*

FICTION

The Dark Room
Popcorn: Hollywood Stories

PLAYS

Public Lives
The Animal in the Trees
Four Roses
Love in the DMZ
Avalon *(a musical)*
The Medium at Large *(a musical)*
Normal, Nebraska *(a musical)*

POETRY

Prayers for the Little Ones
Prayers for the Nature Spirits
The Quiet Animal
This Earth *(also an album with Tim Wheater)*

FEATURE FILMS

God's Will *(writer/director)*

THE WRITER'S LIFE

Insights from The Right to Write

JULIA CAMERON

JEREMY P. TARCHER/PUTNAM

a member of Penguin Putnam Inc.

New York

Most Tarcher/Putnam books are available at special quantity discounts for bulk purchase for sales promotions, premiums, fund-raising, and educational needs. Special books or book excerpts also can be created to fit specific needs. For details, write Putnam Special Markets, 375 Hudson Street, New York, NY 10014.

Jeremy P. Tarcher/Putnam
a member of
Penguin Putnam Inc.
375 Hudson Street
New York, NY 10014
www.penguinputnam.com

Library of Congress Cataloging-in-Publication Data

Cameron, Julia.
[Right to write. Selections]
The writer's life / Julia Cameron
p.   cm.
Excerpts from the author's The right to write.
ISBN 1-58542-103-0
I. Authorship.   I. Title.
PN151.C29   2001   2001018914
808'.02—dc21

Printed in the United States of America

1   3   5   7   9   10   8   6   4   2

This book is printed on acid-free paper. ∞

Book design by Claire Vaccaro and Jennifer Ann Daddio

AUTHOR'S NOTE

It is my hope that this book will dismantle some of the negative mythology that surrounds the writing life in our culture. I have found that life to be positive, invigorating, spiritually sourced, and eminently doable. In my experience, the writing life is a simple life, self-empowered and self-empowering. This book will be a cheerleader for those trying the writing life, a companion for those living it, and a thank-you to my own writing for the life it has given to me. It is my hope that this book will help to heal writers who are broken, initiate writers who are afraid, and entice writers who are standing at river's edge, wanting to put a toe in.

Why should we write? We should write because it is human nature to write. Writing claims our world. It makes it directly and specifically our own. We should write because humans are spiritual beings and writing is a powerful form of prayer and meditation, connecting us to our own insights and to a higher and deeper level of inner guidance as well. We should write, above all, because we are writers whether we call ourselves writers or not. The Right to Write is a birthright, a spiritual dowry that gives us the keys to the kingdom. Higher forces speak to us through writing. Call them Inspiration, Muses, Angels, God, Hunches, Intuition, Guidance, or simply a good story—whatever you call them, they connect us to something larger than ourselves that allows us to live with greater vigor and optimism.

In our current culture, writing is not forbidden; it is discouraged. Hallmark does it for us. We shop for the card that is "closest" to what we wish to say. Schools drill us about how to say what we want to and the how-to involves things like proper spelling, topic sentences, and the avoidance of detours so that logic becomes the field marshal and emotion is kept at bay. Writing, as we are taught to do it, becomes an antihuman activity. We are forever editing, leaving out the details that might not be pertinent. We are trained to self-doubt, to self-scrutiny in the place of self-expression.

Most of us try to write too carefully. We try to do it "right." We try to sound smart. We try, period. Writing goes much better when we don't work at it so much. When we give ourselves permission to just hang out on the page. For me, writing is like a good pair of pajamas—comfortable. In our culture, writing is more often costumed up in a military outfit. We want our sentences to march in neat little rows, like well-behaved boarding-school children. Burn down the school. Save the books, perhaps, but get the teacher to tell you the real secrets: What does he write and read as a guilty pleasure? Guilty pleasure is what writing is all about. It is about attractions, words you can't resist using to describe things too interesting to pass up. And forget lofty motives.

We should write because writing brings clarity and passion to the act of living. Writing is sensual, experiential, grounding. We should write because writing is good for the soul. We should write because writing yields us a body of work, a felt path through the world we live in. Anton Chekhov advised actors, "If you want to work on your acting, work on yourself." This same advice applies to working on our writing. Our writing life, our life "as a writer," cannot be separated from our life as a whole. Start where you are. It's a luxury to be in the mood to write. It's a blessing but it's not a necessity.

Well written—what does that mean? In school it usually means clear, orderly thinking. Neat enough grammar. Lots of orderly facts. It may also mean things we are taught, like "topic sentences" and "transitions." Very often it does not mean words that sing off the page, innovative word combinations, paragraphs of great free associations and digressions—all the gifts a young poet or novelist might have and want to use but not find useful under the scholarly discipline of an academic paper. Writing is like breathing, it's possible to learn to do it well, but the point is to do it no matter what. I believe we come into life as writers. We are born with a gift for language, and it comes to us within months as we begin to name our world. Words give us power.

We put a lot of bunk around the notion of being a writer. We make a big deal out of putting words on paper instead of simply releasing them into the air. We have a mythology that tells us that writing is a torturous activity. Believing that, we don't even try it or, if we do, and if we find it unexpectedly easy, we stop, freeze up, and tell ourselves that whatever it is that we're doing, it can't be "real" writing. What if there were no such thing as a writer? What if everyone simply wrote? What if there were no "being a real writer" to aspire to? What if writing were simply about the act of writing?

Writing is a lot like driving a country blacktop highway on a hot summer day. There is a wavery magical spot that shimmers on the horizon. You aim toward it. You speed to get there, and when you do, the "there" vanishes. You look up to see it again, shimmering in the distance. You write toward that. I suppose some people might call this unrequited love or dissatisfaction. I think it's something better. The act of writing, the aiming at getting it right, is pure thrill, pure process, as exciting as drawing back a bow. Hitting a creative bull's-eye, a sentence that precisely expresses what you see shimmering on the horizon—those sentences are worth the chase. But the chase itself, the things you catch out of the corner of your eye—that's worth something too. I love it when I write well, but I love it when I write, period.

If we didn't have to worry about being published and being judged, how many more of us might write a novel just for the joy of making one? Why should we think of writing a novel as something we couldn't try—the way an amateur carpenter might build a simple bookcase or even a picnic table? What if we didn't have to be good at writing? What if we got to do it for sheer fun? What if writing were approached like whitewater rafting? Something to try just for the fact of having tried it, for the spills and chills of having gone through the rapids of the creative process.

When people undertake writing, it is often not with the agenda of writing but with the agenda of "becoming a writer." We have an incredible amount of mystery, mystique, and pure bunk around exactly what the phrase means. The fact that the act of writing makes you a writer barely enters the equation at all. Instead, we come up with ideas like "Real writers are published," or "Real writers make a living from their writing." In a sense, we are saying, "Real writers get validation from others that they are writers." With a product-not-process orientation like this, is it any wonder that the aspiring writer is seized by anxiety? Even those gifted with a silver tongue doubt that they are gifted with a silver pen. The blank page strikes them like a blank check where they may be asked to fill in too large an amount.

The blank page creates a sense of seriousness. We forget the term "rough draft" and want everything to emerge as well-polished gems. There's no place for error, for colloquialisms, for the charming roundabouts. Our schooling kicks in and we remember all those rules for good writing: topic sentences, organization. . . . Most of us think we can't write. It doesn't have to be like that. If we eliminate the word "writer," if we just go back to writing as an act of listening and naming what we hear, some of the rules disappear.

One of the simplest and smartest things I ever learned about writing is the importance of a sense of direction. Writing is about getting something down, not about thinking something up. Whenever I strive to "think something up," writing becomes something I must stretch to achieve. It becomes loftier than I am, perhaps even something so lofty it is beyond my grasp. When I am trying to think something up, I am straining. When, on the other hand, I am focused about just getting something down, I have a sense of attention but not a sense of strain.

When writing is about the importance of what we ourselves have to say, it becomes burdened by our concerns about whether the reader will "get it"—meaning get how brilliant we are. When writing is rooted in the process of taking down the next thought as it unfolds itself to us, it is less about our brilliance and more about our accuracy. How carefully are we willing to listen? How much control are we willing to surrender for the sake of allowing creativity to move through us rather than our trying to flog it forward for agendas of our own? There is an organic shape, a form-coming-into-form that is inherent in the thing we are observing, listening to, and trying to put on the page. It has rules of its own that it will reveal to us if we listen with attention.

Most of us are really willing only to write well, and this is why the act of writing strains us. We are asking it to do two jobs at once: to communicate to people and to simultaneously impress them. Is it any wonder that our prose buckles under the strain of doing this double task? When we "forget ourselves," it is easy to write. We are not standing there, stiff as a soldier, our entire ego shimmied into every capital "I." When we forget ourselves, when we let go of being good and settle into just being a writer, we begin to have the experience of writing itself writing through us. We retire as the self-conscious author and become something else—the vehicle for self-expression. When we are just the vehicle, the storyteller and not the point of the story, we often write very well—we certainly write more easily.

The brain enjoys writing. It enjoys the act of naming things, the processes of association and discernment. Picking words is like picking apples: this one looks delicious. Writing—and this is a big secret—wants to be written. Writing loves a writer the way God loves a true devotee. Writing will fill your heart if you let it. It will fill your pages and help to fill your life.

The myth that we must have "time"—more time—in order to create is a myth that keeps us from using the time we do have. If we are forever yearning for "more," we are forever discounting what is offered. Often the greased slide to writer's block is a huge batch of time earmarked: "Now write." Making writing a big deal tends to make writing difficult. Keeping writing casual tends to keep it possible. Nowhere is this more true than around the issue of time. One of the biggest myths about writing is that in order to do it we must have great swathes of uninterrupted time.

For most of us, the seductive and unstated part of "if I had enough time" is the unstated sentence "to hear myself think." In other words, we imagine that if we had time we would quiet our more shallow selves and listen to a deeper flow of inspiration. Again, this is a myth that lets us off the hook—if I wait for enough time to listen, I don't have to listen now, I don't have to take responsibility for being available to what is trying to bubble up today. The "if I had time" lie is a convenient way to ignore the fact that novels require being written and that writing happens a sentence at a time. Sentences can happen in a moment. Enough stolen moments, enough stolen sentences, and a novel is born—without the luxury of time.

If we learn to write from the sheer love of writing, there is always enough time, but time must be stolen like a quick kiss between lovers on the run. As a shrewd woman once told me, "The busiest and most important man can always find time for you if he's in love with you and, if he can't, then he is not in love." When we love our writing, we find time for it. The trick to finding writing time, then, is to write from love and not with an eye to product. Don't try to write something perfect; just write. Don't try to write the whole megillah; just start the whole megillah. Yes, it is daunting to think of finding time to write an entire novel, but it is not so daunting to think of finding time to write a paragraph, even a sentence. And paragraphs, made of sentences, are what novels, plays, and stories are really made of.

The trick of finding writing time is to make writing time in the life you've already got. That's where you've got leverage. Stop imagining some other life as a "real" writer's life. Key West sunsets do not make a writer's life. Trust funds do not fund the flow of ideas. All lives are writers' lives because all of us are writers. Taking the time to write in our lives gives us the time of our lives. As we describe our environments, we begin to savor them. Even the most rushed and pell-mell life begins to take on the patina of being cherished.

Perfectionism is a primary writer's block. We want to write—we just want to do it perfectly. Deliberately indulge in some "bad writing." The danger of writing and rewriting at the same time is that it is tied in to mood. In an expansive mood, whatever we write is great. In a constricted mood, nothing is good. This makes writing a roller coaster of judgment and indictment: guilty or innocent, good or bad, off with its head or allowed to go scot-free. The computer, with its deadly "delete" button, should be seen as a clear and present enemy. Most often, a small scrap of writing that we are tempted to send to oblivion can be saved in a "slush" file and found to fit perfectly later.

There should be some artier way of saying it: I think of it as laying track. I believe that what we want to write wants to be written. There are people who worry about how to lay out the best trail. To me, that's a little topiary and advanced. The "best" trail is for second drafts. The getting from point to point, the drive across country, is the first draft. First drafts that are allowed to find their own shape and form very often do find the best trail or something very close to it. Writing that is overplanned and overrehearsed is juiceless. Later drafts, then, are about plumping it up. How much better to have a wild and somewhat unruly first draft, something that can be shaped and tamed, something so full of detail, it's a question of what we want to leave in, not a question of what still needs to be added.

Writing is like listening to a melody line in my head. Note by note, it knows where it wants to go. I follow it and lay it down. I can pare it, shape it, and polish it later. For the moment, my job is just to get it down, just to catch the thought, which I can add to or embellish later on. There is a pattern or form being formed like a crystal in the subconscious of an artist. Growing in darkness by dribs and drabs, over time it makes a magnificent formation. My job is to take down the dribs and drabs—to free-associate, if you will, knowing that the associations have their own plans for where we're going with all this.

Being in the mood to write, like being in the mood to make love, is a luxury that isn't necessary in a long-term relationship. Just as the first caress can lead to a change of heart, the first sentence, however tentative and awkward, can lead to a desire to go just a little further. All of us have a sex drive. All of us have a drive to write. The drive to write is a primary human instinct: the drive to name, order, and, in a sense, control our experience. The drive to write, that primal glee we felt as children when we learned the letters that formed our names and then the words that formed our world, is a drive that has been buried in our frantic, electrical, telephonic age. E-mail is a rebalancing of the wheel. People love e-mail because they love to write. Furthermore, because it is instantaneous, e-mail tricks people into evading their censors.

Doing it all the time, whether or not we are in the mood, gives us ownership of our writing ability. It takes it out of the realm of conjuring where we stand on the rock of isolation, begging the winds for inspiration, and it makes it something as doable as picking up a hammer and pounding a nail. Writing may be an art, but it is certainly a craft. We often make the mistake of thinking that we "have" to be in the "right" mood to write. The truth is, any mood can be used for writing. Any mood is a good writing mood. The trick is to simply enter *whatever* mood like a room and sit down and write from there.

Drama in our lives often keeps us from putting drama on the page. Some drama happens and we lose our sense of scale in our emotional landscape. When this happens, we need to reconnect to our emotional through line. We need a sense of our "before, during, and after" life. You can use your negative feelings as positive fuel. You can base characters and events on the real-life turmoil you are grappling with. Characters that begin with a base in a real person soon enough become characters in their own rights, citizens with their own opinions, denizens of a world that very rapidly seems to be more about their making than writing for revenge. Writing to "show them" is a perfectly fine way to start, because sooner or later what you show yourself is the willingness and invention of your own creativity.

Not wanting to second-guess Virginia Woolf, a woman of firm opinions, I nonetheless want to venture that she was suggesting we need a room of our own so that we could put aside the needs and agendas and dramas of others and concentrate on the actual feat of writing. The trick is, therefore, a psychological door, not a physical one—a door that is really proof against the intrusions of others and their agendas. *Keep the drama on the page.* This deal, simple in the statement, is the key to all serenity and accomplishment as a writer. It's a habit of saying, when drama rears its head, "I'll think about that later—after I write." For a writer, personal drama is a drink of creative poison. Keeping the drama on the page is ruthless, enlightened self-interest. It makes the luxury of a room of one's own largely a matter of convenience, not necessity.

We can use writing the way a filmmaker uses a lens: to pull focus, to put things into a different perspective. We can zoom into a close-up. We can pull way back and put something against a larger swathe of landscape. If writing is observing the movie in our minds, it is also editing it, adding a soundtrack, putting on a voice-over. Acting our way into right thinking is putting pen to the page even when the censor is shrieking. It is choosing to write even when writing feels "wrong" to us—because we're tired, we're bothered, we're any number of things that writing will change if only we will let it. It's letting it that's the trick.

Writing is medicine. It is an appropriate antidote to injury. It is an appropriate companion for any difficult change. Because writing is a practice of observation as much as invention, we can become curious as much as frightened in the face of change. Writing about the change, we can help it along, lean into it, cooperate. Writing allows us to rewrite our lives. When injuries are buried instead of acknowledged, they create a potent writer's block. Lurking in our unconscious, they "mysteriously" leech us of writing power. Made conscious, our creative villains can be actively faced down. Try writing for revenge. Try writing "to show them." You turn the dross of your disappointments into the gold of accomplishment. In the long run, the person you show is yourself.

As writers, as artists, we are often confronted with lint pickers. Most teachers—not all, but most—are lint pickers when they grade papers. All grammatical errors are clearly marked in red, but where are the sentences that say, "This phrase is great! The overall thinking here is marvelous." Most of us never got that kind of feedback, and we don't get it still. We do not see our size. We do not view ourselves with accuracy. We are far larger, far more marvelous, far more deeply and consistently creative than we recognize or know. We do not see or hear our magnitude. Why is this? Seeking to value ourselves, we look to others for assurance. If what we are doing threatens them, they cannot give it. If what we envision is larger than what they can see, they cannot give support for what it is we are doing.

Writing is an act of self-cherishing. We often write most deeply and happily on those areas closest to our hearts. Valuing our experience is not narcissism. It is not endless self-involvement. It is, rather, the act of paying active witness to ourselves and to our world. Such witness is an act of dignity, an act that recognizes that life is essentially a sacred transaction of which we know only the shadow, not the shape.

As a writer, I am always staring at distance, always looking at something moving toward me from a long way off. That focusing is writing. It begins as an image, something I want to see more clearly. Writing then becomes like the act of focusing a set of binoculars and setting down what appears. It is observing and writing something down, not thinking something up. Things do come to us through writing, and they are not always so intangible as insights. Moving our hands across the page, we make a handmade life. We tell the Universe what we like and what we don't like, what is bugging us and what is giving us delight. We tell the Universe and ourselves what we would like more of, what we would like less of, and through this clarity a shift occurs. Writing is a psychological as well as a physical activity. When I "clear my thoughts," I am literally rearranging my life itself.

One of the mysteries of the writing life is the fact that an investment of interest in column A—say, listening to a great piece of music—will pay off obliquely when we set pen to paper on an entirely different topic. Writing is what we make from the broth of our experience. If we lead a rich and varied life, we will have a rich and varied stock of ingredients from which to draw on. If we lead a life that is too narrow, too focused, too oriented toward our goals, we will find our writing lacks flavor, is thin on the nutrients that make it both savory and sustaining. Although we tend to think of it as linear, writing is a profoundly visual art. Even if we are writing about internal experience, we use images to do it. For this reason, we must consciously and constantly restock our store of images. We do this by focusing on what is around us.

Very often work dries up precisely because it was going so well. We have simply over-fished our inner reservoir without having taken the time and care to consciously restock our storehouse of images. An Artist Date is half "artist" and half "date." You are romancing, wooing, courting your creative consciousness. This is something that requires you and your inner artist to spend time alone. Even the smallest amount of self-nurturance will have an immediate and beneficial impact on your writing. A regular and gentle program of self-care will result in a level of ease and authority in your writing that is often astounding.

Writing doesn't always have to know where it's going. In school we are taught to march our thoughts in nice orderly rows—as though that's the way they occur to us. The writing we learn in school is stripped down, chromeless, noncustomized prose. Prose can benefit from a little lurid frippery. The understated, carefully modified, exclamation-points-only-with-papal-permission prose that we learn actually bores a lot of us out of writing. Writing like that—"good" writing—is like watching a movie we've seen before. We can admire the craft, but none of the outcome chills us to the marrow, moves us to tears, or causes us to gasp with recognition. Bad writing—when it's good—is like New York street pizza. Sometimes it's a little too crusty. Sometimes it's a little soggy, but the tang is undeniable. It has flavor. Spice. Juice.

Observed closely enough, all of life is interesting. The practice of writing teaches this. All of life is filled with drama. Observed closely, small moments have large impact. They are like the small variations as we move scale to scale in piano practice. The eye, like the ear, becomes trained to nuance by consistent attention. Just as Bach's "Goldberg Variations" charmed an insomniac prince, our focused attention charms the part of ourselves that is restive and disordered. "God is in the details," exclaimed Ludwig Mies van der Rohe. Writing specifically, writing detail by detail, we encounter not only ourselves, not only our truth, but the greater truth that stands behind all art and all communication. We touch the spiritual fact that as divided as we may feel ourselves to be, we are nonetheless One.

Writing is making choices, and the choices we make can be generic, which will cost us our reader's faith, or specific, which will gain our reader's trust. Detail allows us to communicate precisely what we mean. Being specific in writing means taking the general and looking at it more closely. Sometimes, often, specificity is as simple as facts. "A horse" becomes "a small brown horse with a white star and wispy tail." Each fact adds to our credibility. The reader trusts us because we give enough detail for our eyes—which they are using—to be trusted.

Writing is about living. It is about specificity. Writing is about seeing, hearing, feeling, smelling, touching. It is more about all these things than it is about thinking. We have an idea that "writers" must be "smart." By smart, we actually mean "clever." We know what clever looks like; it is the Maserati turn of a phrase, the cornering of a comment with a speed and grace the rest of us can't handle. Yes, that's one form of writing, the showy kind, but that is not all that writing is about.

Once upon a time we talked about "the love of letters." We don't do this much anymore. I wish we would go back to talking about the love of letters and writing from the love of letters and, perhaps, to writing love letters. At its base, for me, love is what writing is about. As an act of love, it deserves our protection and our deepest respect. Writing is an act of connection, but it connects the writer first to the Self and second to the world. In order to practice self-expression we must keep that in the proper order. We must protect the Self we mean to express. We must treat our writing carefully, as if it were valuable. It *is* valuable.

Writing is communication, yes, but that communication begins internally. The Self communicates to the writer and the writer communicates to the Self. The gist of that communication is what the writer communicates to the world. When the world is allowed to interrupt too early, the Self withdraws. Showing our writing to hostile or undiscerning readers is like lending money to people with terrible fiscal pasts. We will not be repaid as we wish. Our work will not be valued. They will respond in dangerous extremes, "brilliant" or "awful." (Long experience teaches that extremes of any kind, high or low, are dangerous to the writing process because they create self-consciousness.)

As a writing teacher, it is my experience that if I praise a student's strengths, the weaknesses eventually fall away. If I focus on the weaknesses, the strengths, too, may wobble and even vanish. A young writer is like a young horse. The basic gaits must be developed before too much perfection is required. Just as we would not give over a valuable young horse to just anybody to train, we must not give over our work to just anybody to critique. We must write from love and we must choose those to read us who read from love: the love of words. The love of naming our experience must finally be the guiding force in what we put on the page. When we write from fear of criticism, we hamper our stride and we cripple our voice. When we choose as readers those who love to criticize rather than those who love to read, we invite catastrophe.

Gentleness, encouragement, safety—these are the watchwords to be put in place for criticism. I have been writing for thirty years. I have seen more good writing destroyed by bad criticism than I have ever seen bad writing helped by good criticism. I have watched valid and valuable books be picked to pieces by too many editors. I have watched plays start to find their feet, only to be tripped up by too many people contributing fixes. It is a metaphysical law that "the first rule of magic is containment." Nowhere should that law be more rigorously applied than to our writing.

We must be small enough, humble enough, to always be beginners, observers. We must be open to experience, new experience, new sources of knowledge and insight, while still staying grounded in the fact that what we already know and have done is also estimable, also important. In short, we must stay big enough to recognize that any individual criticism, any negative feedback, accurate or not, must always be seen in light of the bigger picture: we have actually made something and we plan to make many—and perhaps better—things more.

Writing for the sake of writing, writing that draws its credibility from its very existence, is a foreign idea to most Americans. As a culture, we want cash on the barrel head. We want writing to earn dollars and cents so that it makes sense to us. We have a conviction—which is naïve and misplaced—that being published has to do with being "good" while not being published has to do with being "amateur." We treat the unpublished writer as though he or she suffers an embarrassing case of unrequited love.

All writers suffer credibility attacks; learning to ignore them is part of surviving as a writer. Based on the idea that writing is product, not process, the credibility attack wants to know just what credits you've amassed lately. The mere act of writing, the fact of which makes you a writer, counts for nothing with this monster. Writing for the love of writing, the sheer act of writing, is the only antidote for the poison of credibility attacks—and the antidote is short-lived and must be readministered.

On a very primal level, writing is naughty. It is an act of self-possession. "This is what I think. . . ." There is an anarchistic two-year-old inside most of us, and that child likes to have its say. When we let writing be about that, when we think of it as sharing secrets with ourselves, gleeful at what we are daring to do, writing doesn't take much "discipline." When writing gets to be a work in progress, when writing gets to be real "live" rock and roll, then writing becomes infectious instead of disciplined. Writing becomes "Just do it" and "Hey, let's dance."

People who write out of "discipline" are taking a substantial risk. They are setting up a situation against which they may one day strongly rebel. Writing from discipline invites extremism: "I have to do this or I'm a failure." Writing from discipline creates a potential for emotional blackmail: "If I don't write I've got no character." People who write from discipline also take the risk of trying to write from the least open and imaginative part of themselves, the part of them that punches a time clock instead of taking flights of fancy. "Commitment" is a word I prefer to the word "discipline." It is more proactive, more heart-centered, and ultimately more festive and productive.

Writing rewards practice. Writing rewards attention. Writing, like sex with the right partner, remains a gateway to greater mystery, a way to touch something greater than ourself. Writing is an act of cherishing. It is an act of love: I love this and this and this. Like any great love, writing is specific—not generic. If we are to write well, we must practice being specific. The specificity of a writer's detail, the willingness to disclose detail, allows or bars intimacy. If I say, for example, that the walls to my writing room are pastel iris and that there are wreaths of dried flowers and Indian corn on the walls, you will know that I am a romantic and a lover of nature and so even my most hard-bitten prose passages will be colored by your accurate perception of my more tender side.

We often talk about a writer having "a body of work" without realizing that this is a literal phrase. Because we think of writing as something disembodied and cerebral, because we "think" of writing rather than notice that what we do with it is really meet or encounter it, we seldom realize that writing, like all art, is an embodied experience. My body, which carries a knowledge deeper than my mind, has answers for me as an artist and as a person. My mind, anyone's mind, for all its multifaceted brilliance, can be a house of mirrors, a maze of dead ends when seeking a creative solution. Writing is a physical as well as a psychological act. Many of our most marvelous writers have been great walkers. There is something about the rhythm of the walk. There is a musicality in motion that spills onto the page.

Our bodies are something more than the cage for our minds. Our bodies are the vehicles of our self-expression. Our eyes, ears, lips, tongue, back, shoulders, thighs, private parts—all of these are writing implements. We speak of "parts of speech." That, too, is another telling phrase. When writing sours from too much writing, a longish walk can sweeten it again. Walking, seeking only to move and in moving "move" something through, I often come to an entirely unexpected idea.

We store memories in our bodies. We store passion and heartache. We store joy, moments of transcendent peace. If we are to access these, if we are to move into them and through them, we must enter our bodies to do so. Entering our bodies, we enter our hearts. "Heart is where the 'art' is." This is why writing by hand, even when it seems clumsy and inconvenient, can lead us to a deeper truth than our flying fingers at the keys. We are "sentenced" to a life in our bodies. That, too, is a telling phrase. Our bodies are storytellers.

The word "conscience" has two parts to it: "con" (with) and "science" (knowing). We cannot have a conscience when we dismember our body of work from our body. We must allow ourselves to be "with" the "knowing" that our body has to offer. This is why it is called not only a "body of work" but a "body of knowledge." True knowledge, authentic knowledge, is something deeper than the mind entertains. When we "reach" for a word in our writing, we need to reach inward, not outward. The body has the word for us if we will just listen to what it volunteers. Touch is incredibly precise, delicate, and powerful; we say we want our writing to "touch" people, but we seldom look at the fact that in order to do so it must embody our actual experience. Our language must be physical. This is how we "touch" our reader.

A sense of place is central to good writing. When we write, we "place" ourselves in our world. We say, "This is where I am right now, and this is how I feel about that." Conversely, when we focus on the places where we have been, we often connect to a deep and specific sense of how we felt when we were there. In other words, by mapping our literal, physical placements, we are often able to more accurately map our psychological placement. Good writers—and good writing teachers—know this.

What writing brings to a life is clarity and tenderness. Writing, we witness ourselves. We say, like our own village elders, "I knew you when you were knee high, and you've certainly come a long way." Writing gives us a place to say, "I miss my dog Ripley. He was so merry and kissy. He was such a buoyant, bonnie little dog." Writing gives us a place to say, "It is two years this week since Dad died. Maybe I should buy some birdhouses like he always did." Writing gives us a place to say what we need to say, but also to hear what we need to hear.

So much of the loneliness of modern life comes because we no longer witness one another. Our lives are led at such velocity that we often feel—and are—quite alone. Ours is a perishable age. We have cup-of-soup meals and entire relationships. We talk on the phone. We say, "I love you. I miss you," but, as the truism correctly has it, actions speak louder than words and the act of putting it in writing says as much, and more, than the words themselves. Writing is old-fashioned, but it helps us to survive and connect in a modern world.

Writing is a way not only to metabolize life but to alchemize it as well. It is a way to transform what happens to us into our own experience. It is a way to move from passive to active. We may still be the victims of circumstance, but by our understanding those circumstances, we place events within the ongoing context of our own life, that is, the life we "own." Owning something also means owning up to something. It means accepting responsibility, which means, literally, response-ability. When we write about our lives we respond to them. As we respond to them we are rendered more fluid, more centered, more agile on our own behalf. We are rendered conscious. Each day, each life, is a series of choices, and as we use the lens of writing to view our lives, we see our choices.

Although we seldom talk about it in these terms, writing is a means of prayer. It connects us to the invisible world. It gives us a gate or a conduit for the other world to talk to us, whether we call it the subconscious, the unconscious, the superconscious, the imagination, or the Muse. Writing gives us a place to welcome more than the rational. It opens the door to inspiration. It opens the door to God or, if you would, to "Good Orderly Direction." Writing is a spiritual housekeeper. Writing sets things straight, giving us a sense of our true priorities.

Writing notices the shifts of direction, the subtle darkening of a mood or relationship. Conversely, writing points out the good things: a new and sunny friendship crammed with jokes, high jinks, and high spirits. "This is a switch," the writing says. "This is really groovy." Our modern lives are vertical with exertion. They are fraught, demanding, difficult. We need someone, someplace, to hear how hard they are. We need, and we must learn to be, our witness.

No matter how secular it may appear, writing is actually a spiritual tool. We undertake it solo, and, not to be too facile, it is worth noting that that word does have the word "soul" embedded in it. Moving alone onto the page, we often find ourselves companioned by higher forces, by a stream of insights and inspirations that seem somehow "other" than our routine thinking.

When writing is perceived as channeling spiritual information rather than inventing intellectual information, writing becomes a more fluid process that we are no longer charged with self-consciously guarding. Instead, we are charged with being available to it. We can "plug in" to the flow of writing rather than thinking of it as a stream of energy we must generate from within ourself. Many people have an aversion to channeling as a word and as a concept. It seems too "New Age" or too nebulous and airy-fairy. And yet, it is essentially a way of talking about the creative process that has been reiterated over and over by artists throughout the centuries.

When we are willing to become gossamer, to allow the fabric of our own personality to expand and stretch to take in what we can apprehend through fully listening to inspiration, we become both more creative and less invested in the authorship of what we can create. Often, we have an experience of awe as we feel what we are creating being born "through" us. The term "brainchildren" becomes more real to us when we experience our creations as entities with lives and agendas of their own. Rather than the "author" of a piece of work, we often experience ourselves as the "midwife" of a piece of work. It is born through us just as our children come through us but are possessed of lives and destinies of their own.

It is possible to write out of the ego. It is possible, but it is also painful and exhausting. I find myself passing on the advice that gave me so much freedom: let something, or somebody, or writing itself write through you. Step aside and let the creativity or the Great Creator or, as my sister calls it, the Great Author do its work through you. In other words, cooperate, don't seek to coopt the power that can enter the world through your hand. You know the picture: the writer as a tormented soul, writing from angst, writing from pain, writing from alienation, cigarette clenched in tight lips, shot glass just at the elbow. The writer is writing from anger, writing from outrage, writing from indignation. Writers do write for those reasons, but they write for many others. Not the least of these is joy.

If writing is about the play of ideas, that word "play" must be given more than lip service. Writing has to have some "play" in it like a bridge cable. Writing has to have some "play" in it, like a jump rope. Writing has to have some "play" in it, like the "play" of light across a field when the sky is dappled with clouds. Writing, in other words, must be large enough, loose enough, relaxed enough to contain all the multiplicity of a full life.

I don't know why the mythology of writers as lone wolves is so pervasive and, for that matter, so persuasive. We do not go into a room all alone. We go into a room that is crowded by our own experiences, jammed to the rafters with our thoughts, feelings, friendships, gains, and losses. Not writing is the lonely thing. Not writing creates self-obsession. Self-obsession blocks connection with others. Self-obsession blocks connection with the self. Writing is like looking at an inner compass. We check in and we get our bearings. I would argue that the writing life is a proof against loneliness. It is a balm for loneliness. It is an act of connection first to ourselves and then to others. Words are formed from "letters" and letters are what we are writing, really. Letters to ourselves. Letters to the world.

How many more books might get written if we believed that writers could write out of love, out of glee, out of bliss—or even out of simple fondness? What if we wrote letters to the editor or to Congress to express our pleasure with the way some things were going? It is my belief that writing is a way to bless and to multiply our blessings. I cherish letters, postcards, faxes, notes, and even Post-its. We are so skilled in the art of negative imagination, we are so adroit at the art of writing out of anxiety, what might our writing and our world look like if we allowed ourselves to inhabit our positive imagination?

Writing, like jewelry design, is a series of choices that lead to a sense of something made—for writers, that something is "sense." Sense brings to the writer choice and, with choice, a sense of at least the potential for happiness. Two variables seem essential for life to feel beneficent. One variable is stability. The other is change. Writing supplies a sense of both variables. Writing both gives continuity and creates a sense of continuity. Writing both gives change and creates an awareness of change. A writing life is therefore—far from what our mythology around writing tells us—very often a life with substantial happiness at its core. Writing to find my happiness, I find my happiness—writing.

You may want to think of this as calling on the Muse. You might consider it a time to involve higher forces. Set pen to page and ask a question on which you need advice. There are no wrong or stupid questions, and over time you will learn how to phrase your questions most effectively for you. Next listen for advice and write down what you hear. Do not be surprised if your guidance feels stubborn, hardheaded, and practical. You may find yourself the possessor of some previously unacknowledged "tough love" wisdom that you can use on your own behalf.

Writing is a valuable tool for integration. The root of the word "integration" is the smaller word "integer," which means "whole." Too often, racing through life, we become the "hole," not the "whole." We become an unexamined maw into which our encounters and experiences rush unassimilated, leaving us both full and unsatisfied because nothing has been digested and taken in. In order to "integrate" our experiences, we must take them into account against the broader canvas of our life. We must slow down and recognize when currents of change, like movements in a symphony, are moving through us.

Writing is about honesty. It is almost impossible to be honest and boring at the same time. Being honest may be many other things—risky, scary, difficult, frightening, embarrassing, and hard to do—but it is not boring. Whenever I am stuck in a piece of writing, I ask myself, "Am I failing to tell the truth? Is there something I am not saying, something I am afraid to say?" When the answer is yes, the writing shows it. There is a softness, a tentativeness, a rot to it that telling the truth instantly dispels. Telling the truth on the page, like telling the truth in a relationship, always takes you deeper.

When we are telling the truth about how we feel and what we see, we find very precise language with which to do it. Words do not fail us. When we are disguising to ourselves and others the exact nature of what we thought or how we felt, our prose goes mushy along with our thinking. Honesty is not only the best policy in writing, it is the only policy that holds up over the long haul. Just as it is exhausting and destructive to lie in our personal lives, it is equally damaging to do it in our writing. It is one of the most frequent fears among would-be writers that they are simply "not original enough." They forget that the root word in "original" is "origin." We are the origin of our work. If that origin is mapped accurately enough, if we are honest enough to name what we find there, then our work is original.

A great deal of attention is paid in critical circles to the concept of having "a voice" in writing. It is my belief that all of us have a voice in writing because all of us have a voice. Working to have a "unique" voice is another concept that gets a great deal of play. I believe that each of us already has a unique voice. We do not need to "develop" it; rather, we need to discover or, perhaps better, uncover it. We talk about self-expression but need to pause and remember that self-expression requires a self to express—and that is what we are excavating when we feel our writing has taken us into vulnerable territory.

Vulnerability in writing is the enemy of grandiosity. It is the enemy of pomposity. It is the enemy of posturing; the enemy of denial. Vulnerability in writing is health, and health—as I can assure you—can be a scary-feeling experience for some of us. Vulnerability requires that we contradict ourselves. It requires that we change our minds. It requires that our perspective shifts. Vulnerability, which is honesty's shy younger sister, is the part of ourselves that renders us capable of great art, art that enters and explores the heart.

Writing well can make us feel temporarily worse because we are breaking the code on ourself. We are shifting patterns we have outgrown. We are shape-shifting into a new form that feels strange to us in its fluidity. We tell ourselves stories about our lives. We believe, "I am this kind of person, not that kind" and then something happens, something jostles us, and we begin, uncomfortably, vulnerably, to wonder, "Maybe I am not so much this sort of person. Maybe I am a little more that sort of person." Pursuing this line of thought, like following the bread crumbs into the forest, brings us to the clearing where the hunters can spot us . . . or brings us to the clearing where the wizard appears.

In a sense, our creativity is none of our business. It is a given, not something to be aspired to. It is not an invention of our ego. It is, instead, a natural function of our soul. We are intended to breathe and to live. We are intended to listen and create. We do not need special pens. We do not need special rooms or even special times. What we do need is the intention to allow creativity to create through us. When we open ourselves to something or someone greater than ourselves working through us, we paradoxically open ourselves to our own greatest selves.

Writing tells us that we are not powerless. Writing tells us that we have choices. Writing tells us what those choices are. Writing tells us when we are shirking responsibility. Writing tells us when we are overburdened. Writing tells us when we love the status quo—"This is a great happiness/ The air is like silk/There is milk in the looks that come from strangers"— and when we want a change. Writing, we effect that change. We are all works in progress. We are all rough drafts. None of us is finished, final, "done." How much healthier and happier if we put "it"—all of "it"—in writing: the flaws, foibles, frills, fantasies, and frailties that make us human. When we connect these dots, we connect.

We write because something "touches" us. We write because we want to "touch" someone else. We write to "get in touch" with the divine or because the divine has somehow "gotten in touch" with us. When we try to write honestly, we speak of needing to "get in touch with how I really feel." We say, "I'm more in touch with myself." So much of what we need, so much of what we want, is to be savored, cherished, cared for, and cared about. So much of what is missing is tenderness. When we commit our thoughts to paper, we send a strong and clear message that what we are writing about and whom we are writing to matters.

When we are procrastinating about writing something or someone, we are always being backed off by our fears. It may be disguised as our business or our "need to focus" or any number of other distractions, but it boils down to our fear of revealing ourselves to others and ourselves. We think we have to be "ready" to write. We think there's no place for showing up dressed come-as-you-are. It is one of the ironies of the writing life that much of what we write in passing, casually, later seems to hold up just as well as the pieces we slaved over, convinced of their worth and dignity. Ease and difficulty of writing have little to do, in the long run, with the quality of what gets produced. A "bad" writing day can produce good writing. A "good" writing day can produce something we later feel needs a substantial rewrite.

As a writer, I love both the act of initial writing—laying track—and the act of editing or rewriting, but I carefully divide them into two separate processes. If first-draft writing is a matter of simply laying track, then rewriting becomes a matter of traveling that track in a handcart, the old-fashioned pump kind you see in old movies. Wheeling along in the handcart, you can see where the joints are missing, where the transitions need to be laid. You look for and fix potential trouble spots before the fully laden locomotive of your readership comes along. Viewed this way, writing and rewriting are two separate but logical processes.

Very often what stands between us and our writing is a desire to be able to write perfectly, to spare ourselves rough drafts and even rough spots. We want to be able to perfectly conceive a final product and write that. This desire to avoid what we think of as dead ends often keeps us from writing. In order to write freely, we must be willing to write less formally. We must allow our writing to be a process that helps us to process. "Write it, you can always change it." This is the rule of thumb for first drafts. This is the starting gate. There is glee in the purity of simply laying track. It's live performance and it's real. After that? It's the editing room: choice, choice, choice.

A writing voice is not a collection of ticks and tricks. A writing voice is a vehicle for communication. The individuality of a voice emerges not by falling in love with your own facility but by learning to move past it. When we focus on having a voice to the exclusion of having something to say, we put the cart before the horse. If we allow ourselves to enter into what we want to express, we will intuitively arrive at appropriate ways to express it. Go back for a minute to the physical voice that we are all born with. That voice rests on a foundation—the breath. We say that a voice is full-bodied without realizing that this is a literal phrase: when we write from our gut rather than from our head we acquire the same resonance that a singer does when the breath comes from the diaphragm rather than high up in the chest.

When we become too complicated, too self-conscious and topiary in our prose, not only our literary voice but our soul itself seems to suffer. "Sell your cleverness and buy bewilderment," the poet and mystic Rumi advised. The best advice I was ever given about writing came to me early in my writing career from Arthur Kretchmer, the editor of *Playboy*. "Don't bother to write for your common reader, Julia," Arthur told me. "You'll never meet your common reader. Write for your ideal reader, the one who will get everything you say." Many of us scare ourselves out of beginning our writing projects by imagining with terror the bad reviews they will eventually receive. I have found that enlisting one Friendly Reader as a "landing strip" can allow me to jump-start a project on which I have been stalled.

One of our great fears as writers is that we will be boring. Give us too much time and we do run the risk of boredom. Give us too much self-involvement and we lose our involvement with the world. Yes, then we are boring. When we center our writing lives on our writing instead of on our lives, we leach both our lives and our writing of the nutrients they require. In order to bloom, all of us need a root system. Just as a regular practice of writing roots us firmly in our lives, a regular life roots us firmly in our writing.

I don't like to make a big deal out of writing. I like writing to be portable and flexible. I like writing to be something that fits into cracks and crannies. I don't like it to dominate my life. I like it to fill my life. There is a big difference. When writing dominates a life, relationships suffer—and, not coincidentally, so does the writing. When writing is about being shut off from the world in a room sequestered with our own important thoughts, we lose the flow of life, the flow of new ideas and input that can shape, improve, and inform that thought. Writing might profitably be seen as an activity best embedded in life, not divorced from it—of course such a view of writing smacks of heresy.

Writers procrastinate because they do not feel inspired. Feeling inspired is a luxury. Writing, often excellent writing, can be done without the benefit of feeling inspired. What writers tell themselves while they procrastinate is that they just don't have enough ideas yet, and when they do, then they'll start writing. It actually works exactly backward. When we start to write, we prime the pump and the flow of ideas begins to move. It is the act of writing that calls ideas forward, not ideas that call forward writing.

At its root, procrastination is an investment in fantasy. We are waiting for that mysterious and wonderful moment when we are not only going to be able to write, we are going to be able to write perfectly. The minute we become willing to write imperfectly, we become able to write. We do not need the courage to write a whole novel. We need the courage only to write on the novel today. We do not need the courage to finish and publish a novel all in one fell swoop. All we need is the courage to do the next right thing. Today's pages may yield tomorrow's play and next month's rewrite, but just for today all we need to do is write.

The Wall is the point where a previously delightful project comes screeching to a halt. The Wall is the point where doubt sets in. No longer writing for the sake of writing, no longer happy just to splash in the pool, suddenly we think about those other people in the pool with us, whether they are faster, better, stronger, showier. In short, we begin to compete, not just create. So how do we crawl under the Wall? Instead of "I'm great," we say, "I am willing to write badly. I am willing to do the work to finish this project whether it is any good or not." When we insist on being great, the Wall stops us. When we are willing to be humble, we wriggle our way under the Wall and back to the glee of writing freely. By being willing to write "badly," we free ourselves to write—and perhaps to write very well. In other words, we go back to sketching.

When people wonder what makes some writing readable and other writing less so, they are centering on the issue of stakes. Stakes are the answer to the question, "Why should I care?" "Why should I care?" is always the question a reader brings to reading a piece of work. Answering that question and answering it promptly and fully is what we mean when we talk about establishing the stakes. For my money, beautiful writing that ignores the question of stakes is beautiful writing that soon becomes boring.

In writing, stakes are a question of clarity and empathy. As writers, we must make it very clear what our characters stand to lose or gain so that our readers, encountering these stakes, can feel empathy and care about the outcome. For those of us trying to write, learning about our own stakes is part of choosing the territory we will write about. I call this finding your "vein of gold." For some people, the stakes that interest them are those of love. For others, the stakes that count are family matters, social issues, financial gain or loss. Part of establishing stakes is not only telling the reader what the potential gain or loss is but also how big that looms in the value system of a character. Very often, when a piece of writing fails to satisfy us, it is because the stakes of the story and the character's value system are at odds.

When we write from the inside out rather than the outside in, when we write about what concerns us rather than about what we might sell, we often write so well and so persuasively that the market responds to our efforts. It is also true that when we see that the market exists for a topic that is high stakes for us, there is no dishonor in writing to that slice of the market. Then we are in the luxurious position of being able to write both from the inside out and from the outside in. It is only when we try writing from the outside in, writing on a topic that has stakes that are not personally compelling, that we run the risk of writing thinly and unpersuasively.

It is my belief that all of us are naturally intuitive and that writing opens an inner spiritual doorway that gives us access to information both personally and professionally that serves us well. I call this information "guidance," lacking another word. I suggest that all writers should consciously and concretely experiment with guided writing. Questions should be posed, and then the answers received should be weighed against concrete experience, e.g., the guidance said this would happen—and it did. It is my considerable experience, based on my own life experience and that of my many students, that an open mind, a spirit of scientific inquiry, and the willingness to delve into the unknown can lead all writers to an unexpected inner resource that will greatly enrich both their lives and their work. This is not my theory. It is my objective experience.

Every time I put my hand to the page, I am altering the energy that flows through my life. "In the beginning was the word," spiritual tradition tells us, and I believe that to be true. "Through every word runs power," advises spiritual teacher Sonia Choquette. "That power is real whether you believe in it or not." "Ask, believe, receive," Stella Merrill Mann shorthands the formula for spiritual manifestation. As writers, we ask questions about a subject, believe what our imagination tells us, and receive very accurate information.

When we become willing to be an empty vessel, we must let go of ideas of how our work should look and should sound. It is the same problem for writers as it is for actors. If an actor has an "idea" of the performance he is trying to give, that concept gets in the way of being true to the moment-to-moment life that is trying to move through him. In writing—as in acting, singing, dancing, any of the arts—perfection is found not in control but in surrendering to the control of the art itself. A dancer will say, "Dance dances through me." A painter will say, "The painting paints through me." Paradoxically we work to control a medium until we have enough control to allow the medium to control us.

As we write, we are both describing and deciding the direction that our life is taking. As we become honest on the page about our likes and dislikes, our hopes and dreams, as we become willing to be clear, the murk of our life begins to settle and we see more deeply into our truth. Writing centers us in ourselves and it moves us out from that center into the world around us. The "I" of the beholder, the hand that holds the pen, writes to get in touch—and touch is profoundly healing. At its very base, writing may be more about touch than it is about anything else.

Wherever I am, whenever I can, I write; I put my hand to the page and my thoughts to the test. Am I balanced? Overreacting? Happy? Sad? My hand moving across the page teaches me my emotional weather. It tracks my moods, my progress, the places where I am "out of reality." It grounds me into specifics, into cause and effect, into perspective. Writing may express the self, but it also quiets the self. It siphons off the busy chatter of distraction and points a way to hear the larger currents moving more deeply in ourselves. In other words, writing allows both the small and the large to have their place.

I am a working artist. This means I am a pragmatic artist. Support from friends is a sensible workable writing tool, and I use it. Some of the best dates of my life and some of the best writing that I've done in my life have occurred on Writing Dates. "Let's go to the coffee bar and write for an hour or two," I have often proposed. There is something enlivening about writing in duos. A great deal of usable track can be laid in chummy proximity.

Multiple writing stations is a cheap trick. It keeps my writer from feeling cornered or like a child being sent to its room. Changing stations with my moods, I bribe myself into writing when I might not feel like it. I write in the kitchen, in bed, on the back porch. Writing in cafes is another cheap trick. Writing stations outside my home help my writer from feeling isolated or punished. So does another cheap trick, the sandwich call. When I feel like I just can't write, I pick up the phone and call my friend. "Stick me in the prayer pot," I tell them. "I don't feel like writing, but I'm going to. I'll call you when I'm done."

I have a drive to write and I do drive to write. I am very aware that the art of writing devours images and that if I am going to write deeply, frequently, and well, I must keep my inner pond of images very well stocked. When I want to restock my images, I get behind the wheel of my car. Driving kicks over my writing engine. Driving lets me write full throttle. Driving drives me to the page. Yet another cheap trick, the Bribe. "If you write another hour, I'll take you out to dinner," I sometimes bribe my writer. "If you finish the first draft, you can get the navy moiré dress."

Writing is the act of motion. Writing is the commitment to move forward, not to stew in our own juices, to become whatever it is that we are becoming. Writing is both the boat and the wind in the sails. Even on the days when the winds of inspiration seem slight, there is some forward motion, some progress made. The ability to show up brings with it the ability to grow up. (We talk a great deal about the fact that creativity involves the nurturance of our inner child, but it also involves the participation and appreciation of our inner adult!) The willingness to face the page brings with it the willingness to face the music. Sometimes that music is a heart-cradling waltz. Sometimes that music is modern and discordant. Whatever the music is, it is what we are dancing to that day. By consciously listening to our daily music, we put ourselves in harmony with reality.

We commit, then the Universe commits. We are the cause; the Universe delivers the effect. We act internally and the Universe acts externally. Again this is where so many of us fall into a false sense of powerlessness. "If I were published, then I'd be a real writer," we tell ourselves. "What are the odds of my being published?" Your odds of being published become one hundred percent the minute you are willing to self-publish. I am, perhaps, more stubborn than most or maybe more uppity or maybe just more convinced of the essential democracy of the arts. I believe that if one of us cares enough to write something, someone else will care enough to read it. We are all in this together, I believe, and our writing and reading one another is a powerful comfort to us all.

It is a very American notion that being paid to do something makes us somehow more legitimate. We would actually do well to take a cue here from the world of sports and realize that just as some of our best athletes are amateurs, some of our most gifted writers may be too. They may never choose to "go professional." Instead of thinking in terms of traditional publication, it serves us to think of putting the work out into the world in as many formats and venues as suggest themselves. It is also true that the moment one commits to self-publishing, the work that is so valued seems to take on added values to other publishers as well. (It's a little like the girl with a boyfriend seeming more desirable because of it, I'm afraid.)

Very often, when people think about writing, they picture the writer's life being best when it contains vast savannahs of freedom— huge bolts of structureless, unused time. I'm not so certain about that. In fact, writing benefits from other commitments. Writing responds well to some gentle scheduling. A day job not only promotes solvency, it promotes creativity as well. The writing life may strike you as "unimaginable." It may seem too hard, too daunting, too confrontational. Like the rocky field, it may look like too much work. But the rewards are solid. The gains are real. And on any given day, you need only do an honest day's words and the rest will follow.

I want to let everybody in. I want us all to write. I want us to remember that we used to write. Before phones, we wrote one another letters. We have been going too fast and we know that. Taking the time to write something down grounds us. Taking the time to write to one another, we find ourselves doing more right by one another. Yes, I want a revolution. I want us to take back the power into our own hands. I want us to remember we have choices and voices. I want us to right our world, and writing is the tool I feel helps us to do it. Writing is an active form of meditation that lets us examine our lives. Yes, writing is an art, but "art" is part of the verb "to be"—as in "Thou art truly human." To be truly human, we all have the right to make art. We all have the right to write.

AFTERWORD

The tool I ask you to undertake now is the most profound writer's tool I have devised or experienced. Called "Morning Pages," this tool is the bedrock of a writing life. Morning Pages bear witness to our lives. They increase our conscious contact with spiritual guidance. They prioritize our days while they miniaturize our censor, allowing us to write more freely and effectively. So what, exactly, are they? Mornings Pages are three pages of daily longhand writing, strictly stream of consciousness. They are about anything and everything that crosses your mind. They may be petty, whiny, boring, angry. They may be cheerful, illuminating, insightful, and introspective. There is no wrong way to do them. Yes, Morning

Pages must be done in the morning. You want to catch your mind before it has its defenses up. You want to surprise it when it's still close to your dreaming consciousness. You do not want your Morning Pages to march like perfect little soldiers, to be a carefully manufactured product of your rational workaday self. What you do want is to catch yourself unawares, to record things you didn't really know you were thinking. Just as walking aerobicizes the physical body, producing a flow of endorphins and good feelings, writing seems to alter the chemical balance of the soul itself, restoring balance and equilibrium when we are out of sorts, bringing clarity, a sense of right action, a feeling of purpose to a rudderless day. Furthermore, writing when we are out of happiness can lead us into writing from happiness. We recall happier moments and we recall happiness itself.

ABOUT THE AUTHOR

JULIA CAMERON, the author of *The Artist's Way*, *The Vein of Gold*, *The Right to Write*, and *God Is No Laughing Matter*, is an active artist who teaches internationally. A poet, playwright, novelist, and composer, she has extensive credits in film, television, and theater.